The Hidden Children of the Holocaust

Teens Who Hid from the Nazis

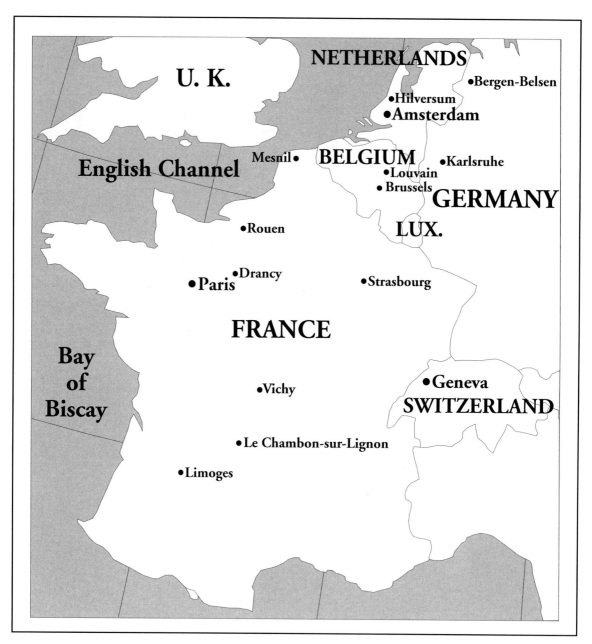

Some of the European towns where the Holocaust survivors who tell their
stories in this book lived and were hidden as children during World War II.

The Hidden Children of the Holocaust

Teens Who Hid from the Nazis

Esther Kustanowitz

SADDLEBACK
PUBLISHING · INC.

Teen Witnesses to the Holocaust

LIBERATION: Teens in the Concentration Camps and the Teen Soldiers
   Who Liberated Them
ESCAPE: Teens Who Escaped the Holocaust to Freedom
THE HITLER YOUTH: Marching Toward Madness
RESISTANCE: Teen Partisans and Resisters Who Fought Nazi Tyranny
IN THE CAMPS: Teens Who Survived the Nazi Concentration Camps
IN THE GHETTOS: Teens Who Survived the Ghettos of the Holocaust
THE HIDDEN CHILDREN OF THE HOLOCAUST: Teens Who Hid from the Nazis
RESCUERS DEFYING THE NAZIS: Non-Jewish Teens Who Rescued Jews

SADDLEBACK
PUBLISHING · INC.

Three Watson
Irvine, CA 92618-2767
E-Mail: info@sdlback.com
Website: www.sdlback.com

ISBN 1-56254-461-6

Printed in the United States of America
06 05 04 03 02 01 9 8 7 6 5 4 3 2 1

Contents

Introduction

It is important for everyone to learn about the Holocaust, the systematic murder of six million Jews during World War II (1939–1945). It is a dark scar across the face of human history. As a student, you are part of the future generation that will lead and guide the family of humankind. Your proper understanding of the Holocaust is essential. You will learn its lessons. You will be able to ensure that a Holocaust will never happen again and that the world will be a safe place for each person—regardless of his or her nationality, religion, or ethnicity.

Nazi Germany added a dangerous new element to the familiar concept of "dislike of the unlike." The Nazis introduced the idea that an *ethnic group* whom someone dislikes or hates can be isolated from the rest of the population and earmarked for total destruction, *without any possibility of survival.*

The Nazis chose the Jewish people for this fatal annihilation. Their definition of a Jew was a uniquely racial one: a person with Jewish blood. To the Nazis, a person with even one Jewish grandparent was a Jew—a person to be killed.

The Germans systematically rounded up Jews in the countries that they occupied during World War II. They built death camps equipped with the most sophisticated technology available in order to kill the Jews. With the assistance of collaborators (non-Germans who willingly helped), they murdered more than six million Jews. Among the victims were 1.5 million children and teenagers. These Jewish children, like Jewish adults, had no options. They were murdered because they had Jewish blood, and nothing they could do could change that.

Such a thing had never happened before in recorded history, despite the fact that genocide (deliberate destruction of people of one ethnic, political, or cultural group) had occurred. In the past, victims or oppressed people were usually offered an option to avoid death: they could change their religion, or be expelled to another country. But the Nazi concept of racism did not give the victim any possibility for survival,

Portrait of a Jewish boy in hiding at a Catholic convent in the village of Oulter, Belgium.

since a person cannot change his or her blood, skin color, or eye color.

A few non-Jewish people, known as the Righteous Among the Nations, saved Jews from death. They felt that they were their brothers' and sisters' keepers. But they were in the minority. The majority were collaborators or bystanders. During the Holocaust, I was a young child saved by several Righteous Poles. The majority of my family and the Jews of my town, many of whose families had lived there for 900 years, were murdered by the Nazis with the assistance of local collaborators. Photographs of those who were murdered gaze upon visitors to the Tower of Life exhibit that I created for the United States Holocaust Memorial Museum in Washington, D.C.

We must learn the lessons of the Holocaust. We must learn to respect one another, regardless of differences in religion, ethnicity, or race, since we all belong to the family of humankind. The United States and Canada are both countries of immigrants, populated by many ethnic groups. In lands of such diversity, dislike of the unlike—the Nazi idea of using racial classification as a reason to destroy other humans—is dangerous to all of us. If we allow intolerance toward one group of people today, any of us could be part of a group selected for destruction tomorrow. Understanding and respecting one another regardless of religion, race, or ethnicity is essential for coexistence and survival.

In this book individuals who were teenagers during the Holocaust share their experiences of life before and during the war and of the days of liberation. Their messages about their families, friends, love, suffering, survival, liberation, and rebuilding of new lives are deeply inspiring. They are important because these survivors are among the last eyewitnesses, the last links to what happened during the Holocaust.

I hope that their stories will encourage you to build a better, safer future "with liberty and justice for all."

Yaffa Eliach, Ph.D.
Professor of History and Literature
Department of Judaic Studies, Brooklyn College

chapter one

Hiding

It is dark outside. The night should have brought you rest; instead, you are awake, shivering, starving and alone, afraid of every small sound, scared to even move. Your clothes are old and ragged. They are the same ones you wore yesterday, last week, last month. Your hair is matted and visibly filthy. You are so hungry you can barely think. Your only thought is of your own survival, at all costs.

In hiding, you have few choices. You cannot speak aloud or say who you are. There are no games here, no neighbors or friends. You don't know where your family has been taken or even if they are still alive. You have no idea how long you will stay hidden. You do not even know if you will find enough food and water to survive.

You are one of the hidden children.

Nazism in Germany

In 1933, Adolf Hitler became chancellor of Germany, and his National Socialist Party (usually called the Nazi Party) came to power. At that time, Europe was suffering from an economic depression. German money was almost worthless. Germany had lost World War I and now was being forced to pay reparations, money owed to nations it had damaged during the war. Many Germans thought that their nation was being treated unfairly. Unemployment was high. The morale of the German people was low.

Hitler came to power promising to make Germany great again. Germans were Aryans, the "master race," he said, and were destined to rule for 1,000 years. He blamed Germany's weakness on a fraction of its citizens, the Jews. Hitler claimed that Jews were "racially inferior" and that their presence weakened Germany. Some Germans agreed strongly with his anti-Jewish ideas. Others did not agree with all of his ideas but hoped that he could make Germany strong again.

Hitler salutes his supporters during his 1932 campaign.

Once in power, the Nazis took away the rights of Jewish Germans little by little. At first, Jews were forbidden to go to the same public places as other Germans. Then they were not allowed to go to school or own businesses. In 1935, Jews had their German citizenship taken away by the Nuremberg Laws. Hatred of the Jews became an official policy of Nazi Germany, and it swept the nation. Although some Jews managed to escape Germany in the late 1930s, many stayed,

Opposite: Trapdoor to a secret room on a Belgian farm where a Jewish teen hid during the war.

unable to flee, or hoping that things would improve.

On September 1, 1939, German troops marched into Poland. The invasion triggered the start of World War II. Over the next several years, the German army invaded many European nations. As a result, the Jews in all lands occupied by the Germans were suddenly in danger. Over the next six years, the Nazis carried out increasingly brutal acts against the Jews of Europe. Most were rounded up and put into heavily armed ghettos, deported to concentration camps or labor camps, or executed. All of this was part of the Nazis' "Final Solution"—a plan to exterminate all of the Jews of Europe.

By the end of World War II, six million Jews had been murdered in a planned, systematic manner. Their six million stories cannot be told, but those of survivors can.

Who Were the Hidden Children?

During this period, known as the Holocaust, Jews in Nazi Germany and Nazi-occupied countries did what they could to protect themselves and their families. Desperate parents even sent their children away to other countries or into hiding, hoping to give them

10

These German children and their families went into hiding in an abandoned mine after the Gestapo ordered them to leave their homes.

a chance at life. These were the hidden children of the Holocaust.

Children were usually hidden in one of two different ways. Some were not able to leave their countries of origin and had

11

to be disguised as non-Jews. Blond-haired, blue-eyed Jewish children were able to "pass" as Aryans. These children were "hidden" because their Jewish identity was concealed as they pretended to be non-Jews. Jewish children disguised as Catholic orphans were routinely quizzed by their rescuers on Christian observance and prayers. That way, if they were ever interrogated by Nazis about their background, they could lie believably. It was still hard for Jewish boys to conceal their identities, however, since unlike most non-Jewish European boys, they were circumcised.

In other cases, children were physically hidden, sometimes with their families and sometimes alone. They hid beneath floors, in barns, in attics and basements, always afraid of being discovered or having their hiding place betrayed.

Often, the people who hid them were too frightened even to provide them with food. They knew that they, too, would be sent away or killed if it were discovered that they were helping Jews. Those in hiding often had to find food where they could. To avoid starving, some ate garbage, grass, hay, insects, or small animals. Most had no place to wash themselves and no way to keep warm in extreme cold. Some children did not see sunlight for years. Some, like Anne Frank, were betrayed and sent to concentration camps.

The teens who tell their stories in the following pages were among the lucky ones. Some of them were physically hidden during the Holocaust, and some were disguised. Others hid in both ways. None experienced the unspeakable horrors of the death camps, where the Nazis imprisoned and killed millions of Jews. But all of them lost family, friends, and a way of life, and all paid a steep psychological price in order to survive.

chapter two

Henriette Parker

Henriette Parker was born in Ostend, Belgium. Her parents had fled to Belgium after a Communist regime took over Latvia, their native country. Henriette was an only child and shared in her parents' active social and cultural life. The family often visited Henriette's uncle in Czechoslovakia. As a child, Henriette learned to speak French, German, Czech, and Yiddish.

By 1937 or 1938, I knew my father was very aware of Hitler's growing power. I listened to all the conversations that were going on around me, but I'm not too sure what I understood. I knew that things were very serious. By 1940, we left Belgium for Paris with another family and tried to reach the United States.

We left our house after receiving a phone call, taking two valises with us, leaving our half-eaten dinner on the table. We did not have any papers, any visas. We arrived in Paris on May 10, 1940, the same day the Germans invaded Paris. The

The German army marches victoriously into Paris, under the Arc de Triomphe.

streets were overrun with German army trucks.

The pregnant woman we were with started to have labor pains. My parents helped her deliver her baby and, by the time we arrived for the ship to America, it had left.

Knowing that Paris was no longer safe, Henriette's family returned to their apartment in Brussels.

Our flat had been broken into and ransacked. Nothing was the same, but at least we were home. A few months later, my father received a letter that we were all to be taken to a work camp. My father started screaming in anger and decided that we would all go into hiding. He contacted a man, Mr. DeSmett, he knew from his business, who came from a very noble family that had connections with the underground. Somebody came to our house to take me, my valise and my doll to an unknown place. I was very scared. I was only eight years old.

Going into Hiding

Henriette was separated from her parents, who paid a non-Jewish family named Dubois to take her in.

I was lonely and afraid. I was left in the house by myself a lot. There was a German Women's Outpost across the street, so I couldn't even look out the window. At great risk, my mother came to visit me once or twice, leaving the safety of her hiding place.

I looked thin and pale, so my parents decided that they wanted me outdoors and out of the city. I understood that my parents were doing all this for my safety, but at night, I couldn't sleep thinking about why I wasn't near them, in a bed next to theirs, as I had been in my home.

Luckily, they got me out of that house, because a few days later, the Germans raided everyone on the block and took away all the hidden Jewish children, at least twelve of them. I never knew there were others hidden on that street. I was really just thinking about my own predicament. I left that house with the man who was hiding my parents.

A New Home

Henriette was taken to the village of Mesnil St. Valise, near the French border. There she lived in the home of a woman named Julia Nicaise, a teacher and the head of the local anti-Nazi Resistance.

I stayed with Mrs. Nicaise till the end of the war. She was my godmother, just a wonderful human being. I felt protected and loved—a sincere part of her life.

French Resistance fighters in action.

But Belgium was still occupied by the Nazis, and Henriette had to be careful.

Around the time of the Battle of the Bulge [late 1944–early 1945], our town was occupied by the German army. As the Germans came in, they brought about two hundred American soldiers with them as prisoners of war. Of all the barns in town, they chose our barn to imprison the Americans. I knew that I had to be very careful around the Germans. Everyone thought I was the lady's niece from Brussels. Only the next-door neighbors and the priest knew that I was Jewish.

The night of their arrival, my godmother went to the back of her barn, moved the hay that was stacked against the building, and quietly opened a small door that had been hidden to everyone. She got every American out of there and into the woods. The next day the Germans rounded up many of the townspeople, blaming them for the escape of all the American soldiers. No one gave my godmother up. I was with the doctor next door in case someone turned my godmother in to the Germans. Nobody said a word about her or about me.

Even the neighbors were nice to me. The wife taught me how to play piano and kept me company. Despite their kindness, I remember crying myself to sleep at night when I was alone and no one could hear me. I missed my parents very much. I wrote my parents from this house and I received letters from them.

It's funny that it never occurred to me that something might happen to me. I thought about being shot and how I would respond to the Germans. I was gripped with fear a lot of the time. I knew I was a hidden child and that meant someone had to hate me a lot in order for my parents to be forced to protect me in this way.

Liberation

Finally, the Americans arrived. They were very good-looking, young and tall, and they all had something in their mouth. . . chewing gum. It was my first experience with gum. They immediately gave me some along with chocolates. There were trucks and tanks everywhere, and everybody went crazy, absolutely crazy. Everybody ran into the streets

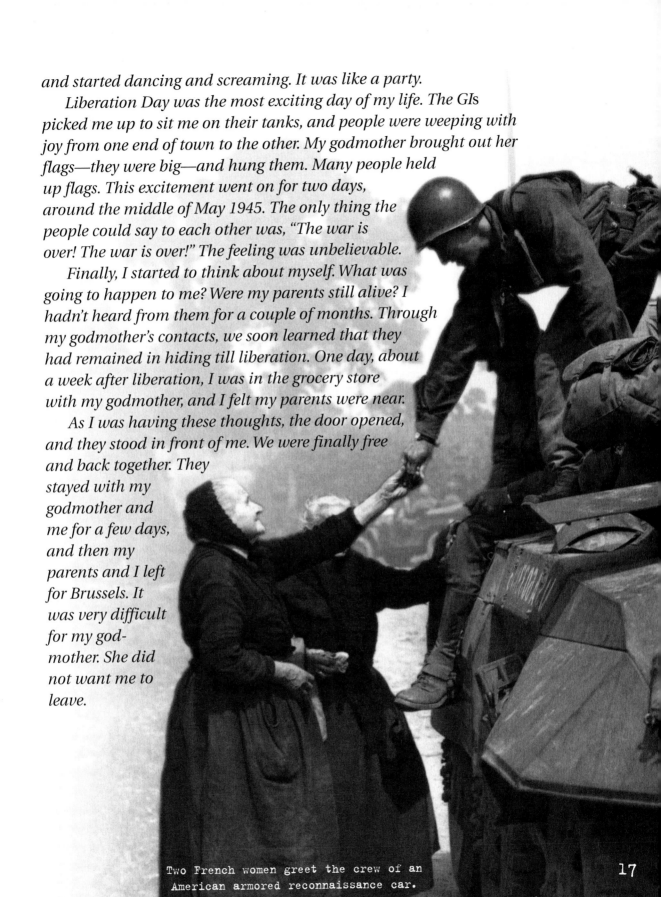

and started dancing and screaming. It was like a party.

Liberation Day was the most exciting day of my life. The GIs picked me up to sit me on their tanks, and people were weeping with joy from one end of town to the other. My godmother brought out her flags—they were big—and hung them. Many people held up flags. This excitement went on for two days, around the middle of May 1945. The only thing the people could say to each other was, "The war is over! The war is over!" The feeling was unbelievable.

Finally, I started to think about myself. What was going to happen to me? Were my parents still alive? I hadn't heard from them for a couple of months. Through my godmother's contacts, we soon learned that they had remained in hiding till liberation. One day, about a week after liberation, I was in the grocery store with my godmother, and I felt my parents were near.

As I was having these thoughts, the door opened, and they stood in front of me. We were finally free and back together. They stayed with my godmother and me for a few days, and then my parents and I left for Brussels. It was very difficult for my god- mother. She did not want me to leave.

Two French women greet the crew of an American armored reconnaissance car.

17

Anne Frank

Anne Frank was born in Frankfurt, Germany, in 1929. After Hitler came to power in 1933, the Frank family— Anne, her parents, and her older sister, Margot— moved to Amsterdam, the Netherlands (Holland).

When the Nazis invaded the Netherlands in 1940, they immediately began to place severe restrictions on the rights of Dutch Jews. Anne's father, Otto Frank, and his business partner, Hermann van Pels, began to make plans to go into hiding with their families. They chose the upstairs back area of their company's building as a hiding place. In July 1942, Margot was ordered to report to a Nazi work camp. The Frank and van Pels families decided to move to their hiding place instead. A few months later, they were joined by another man, Fritz Pfeffer. In all, there were eight people in the hiding place.

Anne lived a more comfortable life than many hidden children. The hiding place was crowded, and the residents did not always get along, but non-Jewish workers from Mr. Frank's business brought food, supplies, and news of the outside world to the hiding place, at great risk to themselves. Anne wrote detailed accounts in her diary of day-to-day life in the hiding place throughout the two years she spent there.

On August 4, 1944, Anne and the others were discovered in their hiding place by the Nazis. All eight were arrested and sent to Westerbork, a Dutch transit camp where Jews and other prisoners of the Nazis were held before being sent to death camps. In September 1944, the eight who had hidden together were sent to Auschwitz-Birkenau death camp. Two of their Christian helpers, Johannes Kleiman and Victor Kugler, were also arrested. One of the other helpers, Miep Gies, found Anne's diary after the arrest and hid it without reading it.

At Auschwitz, the eight were separated from each other. In October 1944, Anne and Margot were sent to the Bergen-Belsen concentration camp in Germany. They spent four months there, living through a brutal winter in unspeakable conditions, before developing typhus, a deadly disease that spread throughout the camps. Margot died of typhus in late February 1945, and Anne died a few days later. Only a month or so after their deaths, British soldiers liberated Bergen-Belsen.

Of the eight people who had lived together in hiding in Amsterdam, only Anne's father survived. He returned to Amsterdam and stayed with Miep Gies and her husband, Jan. Miep gave him Anne's diary, which he edited and had published in 1947. It has since been translated into more than fifty languages and is one of the most widely-read documents of the Holocaust. Books have been written about Anne's life, and movies and plays based on her diary have been made. The honesty, intelligence, and even humor of Anne's writing have made her the best-known of all the hidden children of the Holocaust.

Pages from Anne Frank's diary.

chapter three

Bernard Rotmil

Bernard Rotmil was born in 1926 in Strasbourg, France. His father was an art dealer whose job brought him to many capitals in Europe. His mother was a homemaker. Bernard started kindergarten in Strasbourg, then the Rotmils moved to Metz, France. Bernard's family was in Vienna when Germany annexed Austria on March 12, 1938.

Eight months later, on November 9-10, 1938, the Nazis launched a pogrom, a violent demonstration of antisemitism. It became known as Kristallnacht, or the night of the broken glass. Throughout Germany and German-ruled Austria, people awoke in the middle of the night to the terrifying sound of windowpanes being shattered in Jewish homes and businesses. That night, many Jews were arrested and brutalized by the Nazis.

Up to that point, Bernard's family had been mostly unaffected by Nazi rule. But during Kristallnacht, Bernard and his brother Charles were in the family apartment when a group of about six "brown-shirts," or young Nazi troopers, stormed in.

They were looking for my father. They thought he was the owner of the building, which he wasn't. We stood there terrified. The Nazi thugs— they couldn't have been older than their mid-twenties—began beating

*him
right in front
of us. Then they
hauled my father away.
He was gone for a
couple of days, and we didn't
know what had happened to
him. Then he came back. His head
was shaved, and he wouldn't talk
about what had happened.*

Convinced that they had to leave
Vienna, the Rotmils fled to Brussels, Belgium.
Bernard finished junior high school and began
high school there. In 1940, Germany invaded
Belgium. The Rotmil family fled, becoming part of the
stream of Jewish refugees trying to outrun the Nazis.

Jewish shop owners clean up glass from store windows broken by Nazi
thugs during Kristallnacht, Berlin, November 10, 1938.

Taking Flight

My mother, sister, brother, and I boarded a train to Paris. Our dad had been with us but we became separated. At around 2:00 AM, our train ran into another train near Rouen, France, and caused a huge crash. My brother and I were separated from our mother and sister. We were taken to a children's hospital in Rouen, which had not yet been invaded. I had a dis-located hip and my brother had superficial wounds. We didn't hear from our mother and sister.

The hospital staff evacuated all the children from that hospital because the fighting was nearing the city. They put us on a train to Brittany, France, to get us out of harm's way. We all stayed on Berdère, an island near Brittany which was run by nuns, until the shooting war was over. We stayed there about seven months.

While Bernard and his brother were on Berdère, the French signed a cease-fire with the Germans in June 1940. Defeated France was divided into two zones: the northern occupied territory, which was under German control, and the southern region, which was ruled by the pro-Nazi Vichy government.

The Vichy government ordered everyone to return to their location prior to the hostilities. At that time, we learned that our father was in Brussels. On the way back to Brussels, we stopped at Rouen, where the railroad accident had been. We went to the children's hospital. There we were told that my mother and sister had both died of their wounds, my mother on the day of the accident, my sister the day after.

Home to Brussels

We returned to Brussels and found our father. We even went back to school for a while. By 1941, the Germans had settled in and begun to administer the territory they had conquered. Then they began to arrest Jews. In May of 1942, Jews were required to carry an identity card that clearly stated that you were Jewish. They gave you a little star and told you to wear it. I had one but never wore it. I looked Aryan, so I was able to get away with it. My brother also did not wear the star. He looks even more Aryan than I do, like a real Hitler Youth. I never wore it, but I kept it until I came to this country.

Living in Fear

We never stayed in the same place. We wanted to be a moving target. You heard about your friends getting arrested: They're gone, and they're gone. You heard the slamming door, and you knew that two houses down there was a raid. You just hoped and prayed that next time it wouldn't be you.

The Gestapo would raid early in the morning. They would jump out of their cars and slam the car doors. If you had the timing right, once you heard the door slam, you had just enough time to jump up and take a secret exit.

Opposite: A Jewish man and his daughter walk through the streets of Memel, Germany, as uniformed Nazis in the background laugh and jeer.

Once, my father, my brother, and I were hiding in a house. A group of Dutch Jews moved in soon after. We befriended them. They were very professional, educated, assimilated.

We heard the slam of a car door. It was 3:00 AM. The Gestapo lined us up, and pointed at each of us, one right after the other, and asked, "Are you Jewish?" The Dutch lady turned to me and whispered, "Don't tell them you're Jewish."

I didn't know what to do. If I said I wasn't Jewish and they knew I was, that would be the end of it. They finally asked me if I was Jewish, and I said "Yes." I don't know what happened, but they told me and my brother to go back to bed. I don't know why. Everyone in the Dutch group went to Auschwitz, and none survived.

We knew a young man who always had food and had access to things, and he had befriended us. He was not there the day of the raid, and he never showed up again. He must have been a Nazi plant who betrayed the Dutch Jews. He really liked us; maybe he wanted to let us go. To this day, I don't know.

To this day, when I hear a car door slam, something happens to me. It is something that always stays with me.

Going into Hiding

In July 1943, Bernard's father was arrested and taken to Auschwitz. Bernard made his way to a Catholic monastery in Louvain, Belgium. There, he and his brother were helped by a priest, Father Bruno.

Father Bruno took me to a camp for young boys. My brother was too young to go, so he was placed in hiding on a farm with a family. In camp, I had friends. Some I knew were Jewish; others I found out later were Jewish. Some of our counselors were officers in hiding or part of the underground.

It is hard to describe: We played soccer, but lived in fear. After a while, like a soldier in combat situation, you become immune to it. We talked about who was arrested, who was going to be next. I always hung out with the wild elements and never cared much for school.

My brother and I were so emotionally taken with Father Bruno

Father Bruno and Bernard Rotmil.

and with Catholicism that we asked to be baptized. But he wouldn't baptize us without the consent of our parents. It is unusual for a priest to do this, since Catholics believe that your soul is damned for eternity unless you are baptized.

Some time later, Father Bruno found Bernard work on farms in Belgium, where he was able to hide for the remainder of the war. Bernard's brother was hidden by a family in Brussels. They were reunited after the war. Not until then did they learn that their father had died in Auschwitz.

chapter four

Hanne as a child.

Hanne Eva Hirsch Liebmann

Johanna Eva Hirsch was born in Karlsruhe, Germany, on November 28, 1924. Her father was a photographer who had his own studio. He died when she was only three months old. After his death, her mother ran the business.

Hanne, as she was called, disliked school, even though she had many friends. Beginning in 1935, when Hanne was eleven, the Nuremberg Laws decreed that Jews could attend only all-Jewish schools. As a Jew, Hanne was now forbidden by the government to play with her non-Jewish friends, to attend movies or participate in cultural events. She wasn't even allowed to go to the coffee shop or swim in the community pool. As a Jew, she was stripped of her right to be part of the German community.

In the weeks following Kristallnacht, her mother's photo studio was busy providing Jews with photos for their identification cards, which Jews had to carry from then on. Each ID card had to have the cardholder's fingerprints on it, as well as a photo that showed the cardholder's left ear as another identification mark.

Opposite: Nazi troops oversee the deportation of Jews from the Krakow ghetto, Krakow, Poland, 1943.

In December 1938, new anti-Jewish laws decreed that all Jewish businesses had to be closed.

For the next two years, we lived the best we could. We had curfews, and the hours during which we were allowed to shop were very restricted. As Jews, we were not allowed to hold jobs. Since we couldn't earn a living, we had to live off of whatever we had managed to save. When we couldn't afford rent and food, it had to be paid by the resources of the community.

On October 22, 1940, Hanne, her mother, and her family (her aunts and her grandmother, who was ninety-two years old) were arrested in their apartment. No reason was given. They had one hour to collect their belongings. They were allowed to take one suitcase each. Each person was told to take a knife, spoon, and fork, as well as a blanket and food for a few days. All Germans were living on rations—a set amount of food that they were allowed to buy each week—and since rations for Jews were smaller than that of the population at large, the Hirsch family did not have much food stored in the apartment. They took what they had. After their arrest, they were loaded into rickety old train cars and deported. They had no advance warning. They did not know where they were going. Hanne was sixteen.

Deportation

We were arrested, loaded on a truck, and taken to the Karlsruhe railroad station. It was 6,500 people, I believe, who were deported at this time, from a total of three West German provinces which bordered on France. We were all collected together as families and deported as a group—the entire Jewish population of each of those provinces.

They traveled in old passenger train cars, the doors of which were locked as soon as the people had boarded. They had only the food they'd brought with them, and very little water. The train was bound for southern France, which was ruled by the pro-Nazi Vichy government. The train arrived at Gurs, a French concentration camp located near the town of Oloron-Sainte-Marie.

We arrived at the station in Oloron-Sainte-Marie in the morning. We sat in the train for many hours before we were loaded on open trucks that took us to the camp in the pouring rain. By the time we got to Gurs it was evening, and it was raining buckets. There was total confusion. Most of the adults, including my mother, were totally traumatized. They barely functioned, so the young people had to, and did, function first.

Men and women were taken to separate blocks of the camp. Hanne and the other women were taken straight to their barracks. They walked in with muddy feet, drenched from the rain.

Gurs was a camp full of mud. When it rained, you sank in the clay up to your ankles. The first person from our transport to die at Gurs was an elderly woman. She had been on her way to or back from the latrine that night, which was something we were not supposed to do in the middle of the night. She must have fallen and could not extricate herself. She choked to death in the mud. We found her the next morning. It was awful, but we had already started to see people dying around us. Someone even started to figure out how long it would take, given the current death rate, for every one of us to die.
Our experiences were horrendous. We had very little food and

limited water. We shared our barracks with rats, mice, lice, fleas and bedbugs; we had no beds, but we did have bedbugs. . . . We suffered terribly from dysentery and malnutrition and had no medication for either. The sanitation was awful, and we had constant cold dampness in winter. Even though I had more than one change of clothes, my clothes were always wet from the rain. Soon we had a very high death rate among the elderly. Gurs was the antechamber to hell.

A Door Opens

One day in July 1941, a social worker from a French Jewish child welfare organization [the OSE—Oeuvre Secours aux Enfants, or Aid Organization for Children] came to see my mother. She explained that there was a village called Le Chambon-sur-Lignon 500 or 600 kilometers away. Under the leadership of Pastor André Trocmé, the village had agreed to take in Jewish children from French concentration camps. Would she agree to let me go?

A relief worker in the office of the OSE in Gurs during the war.

Some parents didn't let their children leave. My mother never said, "But I will miss you, I don't want you to go." She loved me enough to give me a chance at freedom, and at survival. I wanted to get out of there, but I knew that if I left, my mother would be alone. (My aunts had already made plans to go to Cuba.) Of course I hesitated, but my mother encouraged me to go. When she asked me whether I wanted to go, I said, "Of course."

Together with six other teenagers, I left for Le Chambon-sur-Lignon on September 7, 1941. Our departure was an official and legal transfer from the camp, and although I felt sad to be leaving my family behind, I was very happy to be leaving Gurs. It was a foggy day, and I remember thinking as we stepped outside the front gate of the camp, how easy it would be for anyone to just walk away into the fog, to fade away and never be seen again.

A Taste of Freedom

Upon arrival from Gurs, Hanne and the others were registered with the police in Le Chambon-sur-Lignon. They were then officially considered legal residents.

After having been at Gurs for almost a year, Le Chambon-sur-Lignon was heaven in comparison. We were free. About eighteen to twenty of us lived in a group home called La Guespy. Most of us went to school. Not all of us were refugees, or Jews; some of us were just children who needed help: French children from poor families, orphans, there was even the son of a missionary from Madagascar. It was a very mixed group. The food was, of course, much better than in the camp. In the beginning, we couldn't eat all the bread that we were given, so we toasted it and made little packages to send back to Gurs.

Our constant worry was what was going on in Gurs. Sometimes we were happy and joking, but always underlying this was our concern about our parents and other relatives.

Opposite: A freight car that was used to transport Jews to concentration camps.

Return to Gurs

My mother's sisters had been able to leave Gurs and eventually made their way via Cuba in early 1942 to the United States in 1948. My mother was not so lucky.

I got to see her one last time. Because my mother had been ill, the camp administration at Gurs gave me permission to visit. But when I got there, the camp was closed to all visitors.

The Red Cross made arrangements for me to see her at the railroad station, about nine miles from Gurs, just before she was deported. I spent the night in the street until maybe 5:00 AM, when I went to the freight yard to see my mother. I saw her through the barbed wire, from a distance of about 150 feet. Someone had told me that deportations were starting, and that she was being sent, together with a thousand other people, in cattle cars to an "unknown destination." It was very emotional; she admonished me to take care of myself and the belongings I had. She told me that she would never come back, but that she thought I was safe. . . . That was the last time I saw her: August 6, 1942. We learned later that the transport went to Drancy, a transit camp on the way to Auschwitz.

I returned to Le Chambon-sur-Lignon with horrible news for my

friends: Most of our parents had been deported in this transport.

After that I said to some friends, "No matter how safe Le Chambon is, we have to leave France and go to Switzerland."

"You are crazy," they said. "How can we do that?"

"We have no choice," I said.

They said, "You're crazy." Okay, I'm crazy.

In Hiding

Hanne was not crazy. Roundups of Jews in southern France, which was controlled by a pro-Nazi government in the city of Vichy, began just a few weeks later, at the end of August 1942.

When the roundups started everywhere, we were hidden by the farmers in Le Chambon. I stayed on two different farms for a total of four weeks. I was with the same girl at both places, but I had never seen her before, and I have not seen her since we hid together. I knew her name then, but now I have forgotten her name, and I have no idea whether she survived.

Young French Resistance fighters in Montpellier, France, during World War II.

One day, the French police came to the first farm while this girl and I were staying there. The farms were so far apart that dogs gave us the first indication that anyone was coming; they would begin barking. Whenever the dogs started barking, we had to hide. We hid inside a woodpile that was intentionally U-shaped. If you pulled out one bundle of wood, there was just enough room for the two of us to crawl in and hide. Then we put the wood back, and there was no opening. Our hearts beat very fast. We were scared. We sat there until the police left and the farmer's family told us it was safe to come out.

Escape to Freedom

I contacted my Swiss relatives, and they obtained a visa for me to enter Switzerland. The problem was, one needed an exit visa from the French government in order to leave France. No one could obtain such a document. Thus, I had to cross the border illegally like all the other refugees. The difference was, once I was in Switzerland, I would be considered legal.

I didn't encounter any border police, but there was a French customs office on the highway about two miles away from the French-Swiss border. I walked by the customs office. A customs officer called me back, looked at my papers, and asked me some questions, including one I was not prepared for: "Are you Jewish?"

Just like that, I spouted Nazi propaganda: "I have nothing to do with that dirty race." Where it came from, don't ask me, it just came. He looked at me with a smile and said I could go. My false identity papers had a different name and birthdate. My birthplace on the papers was Paris. Had he asked me about Paris, I would have been sunk, since I had never been to Paris. Instead, I was lucky. I will never know if he actually believed me, but I was lucky.

Hanne made her way to Geneva, and her aunt took her to safety.

I found myself suddenly back in a normal world, but it was a world that had become strange to me.

chapter five

Henry Wertheimer

Henry Wertheimer was born in 1927. He lived with his parents and sister in Mainz, Germany, from 1928 until 1934, in a large Jewish community on the Rhine River. When his family moved to nearby Frankfurt, Henry went to public elementary school there, taking Hebrew lessons on the side. His father was a wine taster and jewelry salesman, and his mother was a homemaker.

In 1935, when the Nuremberg Laws were introduced, life became increasingly difficult for Germany's Jews. Henry's father moved the family to Paris, joining other relatives who were already there.

Before the War

In Paris until 1939, we were basically free to do what we wanted. In elementary school and high school, everyone knew I was Jewish. They knew I didn't go to school on Saturday because I was religious, and that was accepted.

Before the war things were normal for me—except for an apprehension that something could happen. In smaller towns, things were rationed, but there we never had any famine.

The war started in September 1939, when I was twelve years old. The

French were not happy with the German "alien immigrants" in France, and things got harder for us as Jews. My father and all male "aliens" over a certain age had to go to a camp and work for the French army.

A sign in French and German hangs in the window of a bookstore, denoting it as a Jewish-owned business. Paris, October 22, 1940.

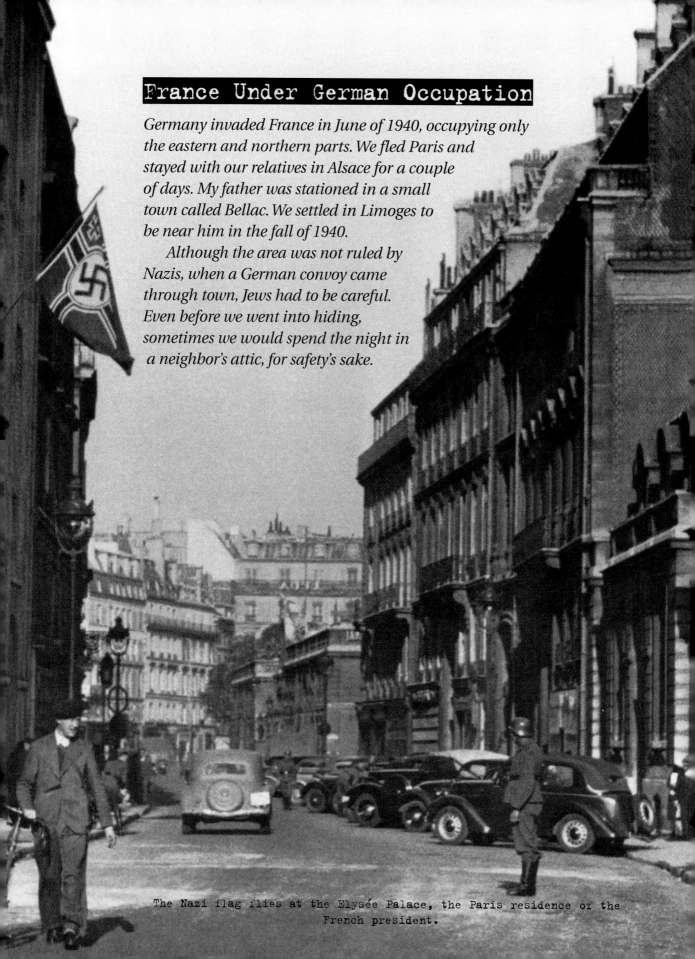

France Under German Occupation

Germany invaded France in June of 1940, occupying only the eastern and northern parts. We fled Paris and stayed with our relatives in Alsace for a couple of days. My father was stationed in a small town called Bellac. We settled in Limoges to be near him in the fall of 1940.

Although the area was not ruled by Nazis, when a German convoy came through town, Jews had to be careful. Even before we went into hiding, sometimes we would spend the night in a neighbor's attic, for safety's sake.

The Nazi flag flies at the Elysée Palace, the Paris residence of the French president.

A New Identity

My father was moved from Bellac to four or five other military camps. Sometimes he was able to come home on leave, but he always had to go back. For every man that didn't come back to work, the French had threatened to deport ten more. In 1943, my father was deported, first to Gurs, then to Drancy. That was the last we heard. We know that from there, he went to the Majdanek death camp.

I went into hiding in February of 1944, when I was seventeen. The rabbi in Limoges got me false papers and a work permit from the French agricultural department, and I masqueraded as a Catholic farmer's helper. The name on my false papers was Henry Weber, the same initials as my real name, so it was easier for me to remember. The farmer and his family did not know that I was Jewish.

A false identity card used by Walter Karliner in 1943–44. At that time, Walter, a German-born Jew who was able to pass as "Aryan," lived in a home for boys run by the pro-Nazi Vichy government in southern France. He used the name William Paul Kiener.

Life in Hiding

On the farm, I lived as a Christian. I went to church and ate everything, even though it was not kosher food. I tried not to go to church, but sometimes, I had no choice. Of course, I had no matzoh for Passover, and I couldn't say the Hebrew prayers like I was used to doing. I couldn't communicate with my mother or sister. They didn't know where I was, and even though I was only about 80 miles away, I had no idea how they were.

The farmer had a wife, a daughter, and an antisemitic son-in-law, who told me that if he ever caught a Jew, he would kill him on the spot. They never suspected that I was Jewish. If they had ever asked me to take my pants down, it would have been a problem. They would have known I was Jewish because I was circumcised.

I lived with another farmer's helper near the farm in a little house with no heat. The water froze in the room. But the farm was in a rich agricultural area, and we ate with the family, so I was well-fed.

Home Again

When Paris was liberated, I decided, "That's it."

Before dawn, I took my belongings and walked and hitchhiked back home. I remember people calling to my mother, "Your son is here!" I had been in hiding for six months.

Opposite: The liberation of Paris, November 1944. Happy young Parisians greet Allied troops.

Charlene Schiff

Jews who were able to stay hidden did not always do so with help from others. In 1942, Charlene Schiff was forced to hide by herself in the forests near her home in Horochow, Poland. She was twelve years old.

After the Germans occupied Horochow, in 1941, Charlene's father was arrested and taken away along with other leaders of the Jewish community; the family never saw him again. The town's remaining Jews were confined in a ghetto. Many died from hunger and disease; others were deported to concentration camps. Charlene's mother knew that the family had to get out of the ghetto if they were to survive. She found a farmer who was willing to hide her and Charlene. In the confusion of their escape from the ghetto, Charlene and her mother were separated. Charlene made her way to the farm alone.

When the farmer saw me, he led me to the barn and I asked him if my mother was there. He said no. I said that I would wait till she arrived, and he said, "No, I'll feed you, you will wait till it gets dark and then you better leave." I looked at him and said, "You made an agreement with my mother." He said, "I changed my mind" and told me that I would have to go when it gets dark, or he would report me to the authorities. He was wearing farmers' coveralls, and in the pocket, I saw my father's gold pocket watch, which I am sure was part of his payment for agreeing to hide us.

That evening, he didn't even come out. His wife brought me an apple and said I had to leave. I was so bewildered that I wandered on the main street of the village, not even realizing how dangerous that was. If there was a God, He must have been with me because I walked on the main road and didn't encounter anyone.

Finally I ended up in the wheat fields on the farmer's property. I sat down in the middle of the fields and stayed there for two days. I finished my food and tried to gather my thoughts. I decided to find my mother, and that was when my odyssey really began. I felt that my mother was waiting for me in one of the surrounding forests and I had to find her.

I started to walk towards the forests.

When you look at a forest, it looks so close, but when you try to reach it, it is much further than you thought. I walked most of the nights and hid in the forests during the day. I was hungry, so I had to find forests that were near villages where I could sneak into a garden and steal a potato or something to eat to keep me from dying of hunger. The beginning was very painful, almost like I was in a daze.

40

Germans executing Jews in a forest near Bochnia, Poland.

I encountered stragglers who had escaped from other ghettos, and we sat around exchanging information, trying to see if they knew anything about my loved ones and vice versa. We were just glad to see other human beings.

Suddenly, there were some children playing and they noticed us and they started screaming "Jew, Jew," and ran back to the village. They wanted to report us and get the small remuneration that there was for finding us. We tried to run into the forest to hide, but this forest had very little underbrush, and we couldn't find a place to hide. Finally, we all hid in a huge haystack, the size of a barn. Soon, we heard that the children had returned with adults. They kept pushing their pitchforks into the haystack. As the people hiding with me were injured, I heard their screams. I waited until it was completely quiet for a long time, and then I made my way out of the haystack, and saw six bodies lined up very neatly there, mutilated. They were all undressed, shoes taken away. . . . I didn't even cover them, I just walked away into the forest.

There was no place to hide along the ground, so I climbed into a tree. This was lucky, because the next morning, that forest was full of Germans and Ukrainians who were having some sort of picnic. I sat there in the tree trying not to move all day long. It was really torture because the trees were evergreens, and they hurt. I even went to the bathroom just like that, from the tree.

When night fell and the people left, I climbed down and walked till I reached another forest.

Charlene hid in the forests until late in the war, when she was found by Russian soldiers. They took her to a hospital and cared for her until the war was over.

My life in the forest is very hard to analyze. I think what kept me going was my quest, searching for my mother. Deep in my heart, I probably knew I would never find her, but if I had admitted that, I would have given up, and I had to go on.

How I lived in the forests, I don't know. But when one is hungry and demoralized, one becomes inventive. I ate worms, bugs, wild mushrooms which I am sure were poisonous. I drank water from puddles, snow, anything I could get. I ate raw rats, when I could find them. Apparently I wanted to live very badly.

chapter six

Yvonne Kray Sokolow

Yvonne Kray Sokolow was born in Berlin, Germany, in 1927. Although she was very young at the time, Yvonne knew that Hitler's antisemitic policies were the reason her family fled to Paris in 1933.

Her father worked in the glass business, and her mother was his secretary. In 1938, Yvonne's parents divorced, and she and her sister went to Amsterdam, the Netherlands, with their mother. Their father remained in France. They thought that the boundaries of these countries would protect them from what was happening in Germany.

In the Netherlands, Yvonne adapted to a new school and a new language, Dutch. Luckily, she was good at

Yvonne after the war, at Columbia University, New York, 1948.

languages. She also liked geography and history, and she played volleyball and softball.

In 1940, the Germans invaded Holland, and by 1941 they had begun to pass anti-Jewish legislation.

Anti-Jewish Laws

Suddenly, we couldn't attend regular schools anymore. We had to begin wearing yellow stars. We weren't allowed to take public transportation. As a result of these laws, I lost my non-Jewish friends. Your friends are the ones you are with in school. My other friendships kind of fell away.

Some of us didn't know who else was Jewish. When we had to wear the stars that said "Jew," that is when we first knew. People would stop on the street and say, "You too?"

Then the deportations started. That was the worst thing. My friends started disappearing. Every morning I used to look out the window to see my two friends who picked me up for school. One day I looked out the window and saw only one of my friends. I knew my closest friend had been arrested.

Nazi guards
survey Jewish
prisoners in the
Warsaw ghetto,
Warsaw, Poland.

43

The class got smaller every day. People were gone not because of the flu; you knew that you would probably never see them again. They had either been deported or had gone into hiding, we never knew which. Some information was trickling to us from Westerbork, a Dutch transit camp. We knew that people were being sent "on transport" and not coming back.

One day my grandparents were arrested. We were living with them. The Germans didn't take us on the same day because we weren't on the list. My grandfather was too old to go into hiding, and my grandmother, who was thirteen years younger, wouldn't leave him. We had to take them both to the Gestapo station. It was horrible. We knew that with them, at that age, that was it; we would never see them again.

After that, my mother found out approximately when we were going to be on the list for arrest, and we stayed another nine months, until 1943. Sometimes, the Nazis deviated from their lists and randomly rounded everyone up from a certain part of town, so it was lucky that we were not taken that way.

When my mother told us that we would be going into hiding, I said that I wouldn't go—that I would rather be deported to a concentration camp like the rest of my friends were. Can you imagine saying such an awful thing? The thought that I would have to just sit in a room hiding was just unimaginable to me; anything seemed better.

When I actually went into hiding, I was ready. By that time, practically everyone I knew was gone.

On the Run

The name on my false papers was Johanna Kuypers. Everything was different on our IDs—name, date and place of birth, etc.—and we had to memorize the information in case we were caught and interrogated.

The underground network, or the Resistance, found us our hiding places. Our first place was in a very small apartment in Amsterdam that belonged to some middle-class workers. We were there for three months. We slept on mattresses on the floor, and during the day we could not move around at all, because the neighbors might see us. We

44

could not go near the windows, and if we used the bathroom, we couldn't flush, or people might hear us. When it became too dangerous for us to stay there, my sister hid with her fiancé, and my mother and I went to a town called Hilversum.

Hilversum was a disaster. We spent a year and a half in four different hiding places.

First we stayed in the attic of a woman whose husband was in jail. Her sister-in-law lived with her and dated German soldiers.

One night, she told one of these soldiers about us, hoping that he could get our ration coupons and use them for her. He terrorized us, saying he knew we were Jews. He stole our few possessions and screamed at us all night. He told us to report to the Nazi police station the next morning. We couldn't report to the station, so we ran to the house of a family we had met through the Resistance, and they hid us temporarily until they could find us another place.

In the next hiding place, we lived with a mentally ill woman. She had imaginary fights with a son who wasn't living there. Her boyfriend hated Jews. We stayed in an attic but could go out a little at night after dark.

Then another family took us in, where the man of the house was able to get food for his family, but not for us. We were allowed to eat only what was left over in the kitchen: soup made mainly of potato peels, and bread that was like cement. I still remember the smell of the bacon and eggs that the family ate at the heated end of the room while we were starving and freezing at the other end.

Part of the Resistance

Our next hiding place in Hilversum was with a non-Jewish family that was involved in the Resistance movement. I was only sixteen, but I wanted to participate a little in the Resistance. There was a center that printed illegal newspapers. These papers contained real news of the war's progress as reported by the BBC. The papers were delivered to one family's house. My job was to pick them up from there and distribute them to a list of other people in the Resistance. I went to these houses with the newspapers stuffed inside my jacket.

Once I arrived at a house to deliver a paper, and I rang the doorbell. The Gestapo answered the door. They had apparently requisitioned the house that morning, and the family didn't have time to warn me. Thank God I hadn't taken the newspapers out yet! I was lucky. Usually I did, but this time I didn't.

I asked, "Does the so-and-so family live here anymore?"

"No," they answered.

"Do you know where they went?" I asked.

"No," they said. I walked away as calmly as I could. I was terrified. My knees were shaking, and I was practically collapsing—it was a very close call.

A Visit from the Gestapo

The Gestapo came to search the house where my mother and I were hiding. They arrived just after my mother and I had finished rehearsing our story about why we were not in Amsterdam. The Gestapo put us in separate rooms and interrogated us. Our stories matched, and they seemed satisfied that our papers were legal and that we were not Jewish. But if they had looked at the papers carefully, they would have known who we were.

Then we went back to Amsterdam, where we hid until the end of the war. Nobody there had enough to eat either, but the woman we stayed with was nice to us. She had very little, but she shared what she had.

I used a false identity for two years. After the war, I had trouble remembering my real name.

Opposite: A church attic in Gilleleje, Denmark where the Gestapo caught eighty hidden Jewish refugees, who were then deported to Theresienstadt concentration camp.

Conclusion

The hidden children of the Holocaust had experiences different from those of other survivors. After the war, some hidden children who told their stories were not believed. Other Holocaust survivors sometimes dismissed the experiences of the hidden children because they had not lived in ghettos or survived the camps. But as Yvonne Sokolow observes, "Everyone is left with scars."

Life After the War

Henriette Parker kept in touch with Julia Nicaise, her godmother and protector, after the war.

"We always kept in touch, and I visited her every Easter and she came to us every Christmas till I left Europe for America. She was a very important person in my life. I lived to experience liberation because of her. She saved my life," Henriette says.

Henriette lives in New York City, where she leads an active life. She speaks in public about how her life during the war affected her. She realizes that perfect strangers can be loving and selfless even as others, at the same moment, try to destroy an innocent young child.

In 1945, Bernard Rotmil left the Belgian farm where he had been hiding and was reunited with his brother. Their parents and sister were dead. Soon after liberation, they discovered that their aunt

Opposite: Group portrait of Jewish children at the OSE home in Aspet, France. The children were brought to the home from French transit camps.

lived in Peekskill, New York. They moved there to join her. Today, Bernard is a writer, sculptor, and corporate accountant.

"The main cause of Nazism was irrationality," Bernard observes. "Democracy and freedom of religion create a sane, rational world. Once logic and reason break down, anything can happen. People believed theories of an international Jewish conspiracy. People thought that if they didn't murder Jews, Jews would murder them. It was totally irrational, but they believed it. In a climate like that, you have Nazism and racism.

"I have painful memories. I had bad moments. I escaped lots of times by the skin of my teeth," Bernard recalls. "But I was lucky. I had Father Bruno. I lived in Belgium. I had a good life after the war. I raised a family, and everything turned out all right."

Hanne Hirsch had met Max Liebmann when they were both in Gurs. They were married on April 15, 1945, in Geneva, Switzerland. On May 8, they heard the announcement of the armistice. "There were no hoorays," Hanne remembers. "We had lost our parents and other relatives. We were all very sober, and rather depressed. The mountains were beautiful. The sun was shining. Everything was the same for the people around us, but for us everything had changed."

Hanne, Max, and their daughter were able to come to the United States in March 1948. Today she volunteers at the Holocaust

Resource Center and Archives at Queensborough Community
College. She also speaks about her experiences during the war.

"One day, long after the war, Madame Trocmé, the pastor's wife,
asked if we had been happy in Le Chambon-sur-Lignon. I never
really gave her an answer, because first I had to figure it out myself.
We were happy to be there, to be safe. Were we happy people? No.
There is a big difference. We had too many worries about our
parents and all that was happening. We had moments when we
were like normal teenagers, having snowball fights or going
swimming, but these were short, fleeting moments.

"Pastor Trocmé was one of the conscientious objectors and a

A soldier hugs two Women's Army Corps members in celebration of the
end of the war, France, 1945.

very principled person. Not many people like him exist. His leadership, along with that of Pastor Thiess, inspired the community to save about five thousand people during this time. What they did was and will remain a shining example of what people are capable of achieving."

After the war, Henry Wertheimer was gladly welcomed by his mother and sister in Limoges. He recalls his feelings at that time. "I felt very disappointed with religion. I wondered, 'If there is a God, then why was my father deported?' I was ready to throw everything away when it came to religion. This probably happened to many people. My religious crisis was probably only for a few weeks, when I was not with my mother."

In April 1946, one of his uncles, who lived in the United States, brought Henry, his mother, and his sister to America. Henry arrived on April 14, 1946, the day before Passover. He was nineteen.

Today, Henry is the vice president of a residential real estate company and is active on his synagogue's board of directors. Several years after the war, Henry returned to France for a visit.

"I have warm feelings toward the French. I lived there for eleven years and never had a problem with them. We were in an area where we could practice religion. There was little antisemitism. We could eat. While I was on the farm, our neighbors hid my mother and sister. That is why I went back last year with my wife. I spoke to some people on the road and asked about the family I had hidden with. They still lived there, but I didn't want to see them. What would I say? 'I was hiding with you'?

"What was most difficult for me is not what I went through but the fact that I lost my father, and why. I felt that he almost volunteered to be deported by not staying back."

Yvonne Sokolow was seventeen when the war was over. She and her family had no nationality. Her aunt and uncle, who had escaped to the United States through Portugal in 1940, helped them arrange for their immigration to America in 1947.

"When I first came here, I felt a culture shock and a loss of childhood. I felt totally alienated by people who asked me, 'Did you go to your high school prom?' High school prom? It made me feel really different. At that time, people just didn't talk about the war experience. All I said about it was, 'I am from Holland.' Not until I met my husband did I really start to talk about it.

"I took my sons to the Netherlands and showed them where we lived. My husband took them to the Anne Frank house. I didn't go. My sister's close friend had lived around the corner from Anne. Anne was one class below mine; we all used to play together. No one else is going to show me the Anne Frank house. I was too close to the whole thing.

"It took me until about two years ago to return to that street. I went by myself, but I shouldn't have: I saw the faces of people who are just gone. You remember it even more when you go back.

A recent photo of Yvonne Sokolow.

"My sons think that I was a hero, which I wasn't at all. I just did what I had to, to survive. I will never say about a restaurant, 'I can't eat here,' because it is never as terrible as what I ate during the war. My sons would open up the refrigerator and say, 'There is nothing to eat here,' and I would say, 'You don't know what nothing to eat is like.' I immediately realized it was ridiculous. How could they? Why should they? But that is the kind of craziness that you are left with."

Today, Yvonne has retired from her physical therapy career. She has spoken in schools and in her community.

Bringing Hidden Children Together

The hidden children have begun joining together. In 1991 the first Hidden Child Gathering was held. It was a great success. Soon after, the Hidden Child Foundation was established, with support from the Anti-Defamation League. Its goal is to bring hidden children together from across the world and to give them a community that can share and understand their experiences.

How the hidden children live now is, in great part, a result of how they survived the war. Every day demands courage from survivors to continue to live their lives despite their history, or because of it.

Those who are able to tell their stories, to bear witness, possess extraordinary strength. For others, the past is too painful. They want to pass on the message that a Holocaust should never happen again, but to tell their tale means to recall a time when survival was an hour-by-hour struggle. The sadness can be overwhelming.

For those who can bear witness, their stories become a necessary and important part of human history. As Bernard Rotmil observes: "Twenty years from now people will say, 'Things couldn't have been that bad, you must have been exaggerating.'

"And the sad part of it is, it was worse than you can ever put into words."

timeline

January 30, 1933	Adolf Hitler is appointed chancellor of Germany
March 23, 1933	Dachau, the first concentration camp, is built to hold political opponents of Nazis in Germany
April 1, 1933	Nazis proclaim a day-long boycott of Jewish-owned businesses
July 14, 1933	Nazis outlaw all other political parties in Germany; a law is passed allowing forced sterilization of Roma and Sinti (Gypsies), mentally and physically disabled Germans, African-Germans, and others
January 26, 1934	Germany and Poland sign Non-Aggression Pact
August 1, 1935	"No Jews" signs appear in Germany forbidding Jews from stores, restaurants, places of entertainment, etc.
September 15, 1935	German parliament passes the Nuremberg Laws
March 13, 1938	Germany annexes Austria
September 29, 1938	Munich Conference: Britain and France allow Hitler to annex part of Czechoslovakia in order to prevent war
November 9–10, 1938	Kristallnacht (looting and vandalism of Jewish homes, businesses, and synagogues) occurs throughout Germany and Austria; many Jews are sent to concentration camps
March 15, 1939	Germany invades all of Czechoslovakia

August 23, 1939	Germany and Soviet Union sign non-aggression pact
September 1, 1939	Germany invades western Poland
September 2, 1939	Great Britain and France declare war on Germany
September 17, 1939	Soviet Union invades eastern Poland
Spring 1940	Germany invades Denmark, Norway, Holland, Luxembourg, Belgium, and France
March 24, 1941	Germany invades North Africa
April 6, 1941	Germany invades Yugoslavia and Greece
June 22, 1941	Germany invades western Soviet Union
July 31, 1941	Reinhard Heydrich appointed to carry out the "Final Solution" (extermination of all European Jews)
Fall 1941	*Einsatzgruppen* (mobile killing squads) massacre Jews in western Soviet Union
December 7, 1941	Japan bombs Pearl Harbor; United States enters World War II
January 20, 1942	Wannsee Conference: Nazi leaders meet to design "Final Solution"
Spring & Summer, 1942	
	Many Polish ghettos emptied; residents deported to death camps
February 2, 1943	German troops in Stalingrad, Soviet Union, surrender; the Allies begin to win the war
June 11, 1943	All ghettos in Poland and Soviet Union are to be emptied and residents deported to death camps
March 19, 1944	Germany occupies Hungary
January 27, 1945	Soviet troops liberate the death camp at Auschwitz
June 6, 1944	D-Day: Normandy Invasion by the Allies
May 7, 1945	Germany surrenders to the Allies; war ends in Europe

glossary

annex To incorporate a territory within the domain of a state.

antisemitism Hatred toward or bias against the Jewish people.

Aryan According to Nazi ideology, a person of Nordic or Germanic background, a member of Hitler's "master race."

Auschwitz-Birkenau A Nazi death camp near Cracow, Poland, where more than 2 million Jews were murdered.

concentration camp A camp where people are imprisoned and kept in inhumane conditions, and may be killed by starvation, exhaustion, disease, or execution.

death camp A camp set up to kill people and dispose of their bodies.

deportation The forced removal of people from one country or area to another.

immigration Moving to one country after having left another.

Final Solution The term used by Nazis for their systematic plan to murder the entire Jewish population of Europe.

Gestapo The Nazi secret state police.

ghetto A part of a city set aside by the Nazis to contain only Jews, which was heavily guarded and lacking in food, water, heat, housing, and health care.

Hitler Youth A Nazi youth group in which young boys were taught Nazi ideology and trained to become soldiers.

Holocaust The extermination of six million Jews and millions of others during World War II.

kosher Prepared according to Jewish dietary laws.

Kristallnacht A Nazi-organized demonstration of violence against the Jews of Germany and Austria on the night of November 9, 1938.

Nazi The political party that ruled in Germany (1933–1945); full name: National Socialist German Workers' Party.

Nuremberg Laws German laws passed on September 15, 1935, that legalized antisemitism and stripped Jewish Germans of many rights.

pogrom An unprovoked attack on Jews by non-Jews, usually involving beatings, destruction of property, and murder. Pogroms occurred throughout Europe from the Middle Ages until after World War II. They were especially common in Russia and Eastern Europe during the 19th and early 20th centuries.

rations The amount of food people are allowed during a given period in wartime.

refugees People who have been forced to flee their homes and seek safe shelter elsewhere.

Resistance Organized opposition, often in secret, to the ruling political party or leader.

synagogue A Jewish house of worship.

transit camp A camp at which prisoners were kept before being deported to death camps or other concentration camps.

typhus A highly contagious disease that is usually fatal if not treated.

underground A network of organizations, usually secret, that act in opposition to the ruling political party or leader.

Vichy A city in southwestern France, where the pro-Nazi government of non-occupied France was based.

World War I The war in Europe that lasted from 1914 until 1918.

World War II The most devastating war in human history, it lasted from 1939 until 1945 and involved countries all over the world.

For Further Reading

Altschuler, David A. *Hitler's War Against the Jews.* West Orange, NJ: Behrman House, 1978.

Bachrach, Susan D. *Tell Them We Remember: The Story of the Holocaust.* New York: Little, Brown & Co., 1994.

Drucker, Malka, and Michael Halperin. *Jacob's Rescue: A Holocaust Story.* New York: Bantam Doubleday Dell, 1993

Eisenberg, Azriel. *The Lost Generation: Children in the Holocaust.* New York: Pilgrim Press, 1982.

Fogelman, Eva. *Conscience and Courage: Rescuers of Jews During the Holocaust.* New York: Doubleday, 1995.

Frank, Anne. *Diary of a Young Girl: The Definitive Edition.* New York: Doubleday, 1995.

Holliday, Laurel. *Children in the Holocaust & World War II: Their Secret Diaries.* New York: Washington Square Press, 1994.

Jules, Jacqueline. *The Grey Striped Shirt: How Grandma and Grandpa Survived the Holocaust.* Los Angeles: Alef Design, 1994

Marks, Jane. T*he Hidden Children: The Secret Survivors of the Holocaust.* New York: Ballantine Books, 1993.

Matas. Carol. *Daniel's Story.* New York: Simon and Schuster, 1996.

Reiss, Johanna. *The Upstairs Room.* New York: HarperCollins, 1972.

Shulman, William L. *Voices and Visions: A Collection of Primary Sources.* Woodbridge, CT: Blackbirch Press, 1998.

Volavková, Hana. *I Never Saw Another Butterfly: Children's Drawings and Poems from Terezin Concentration Camp.* New York: Schocken Books, 1994.

Vos, Ida. *Hide and Seek.* Boston: Houghton Mifflin, 1991.

For Advanced Readers

Baumel, Judith Tydor. *Unfulfilled Promise: Rescue and Resettlement of Jewish Refugee Children in the United States, 1934–1945.* Juneau, AK: Denali Press 1990.

Dawidowicz, Lucy S. *The War Against the Jews.* New York: Holt, Rinehart, and Winston, 1975.

Dwork, Deborah. *Children with a Star.* New Haven, CT: Yale University Press, 1991.

Edelheit, Abraham J. and Herschel Edelheit. *History of the Holocaust: A Handbook and Dictionary.* Boulder, CO: Westview Press, 1994.

Gilbert, Martin. *The Holocaust: A History of the Jews of Europe During the Second World War.* New York: Henry Holt & Co., 1985.

Meltzer, Milton. *Rescue: The Story of How Gentiles Saved Jews in the Holocaust.* New York: Harper and Row, 1988.

Noakes, J. and Pridham, G. *Nazism: A History in Documents and Eyewitness Accounts, Vol. I and II.* New York: Pantheon Books, 1984.

Videos

Dear Kitty
An account of the life of Anne Frank, the best known of all hidden children, this film combines film footage from the Holocaust with photos from the Frank family album and readings from Anne's diary. (Available from Anne Frank Center, 106 East 19th Street, New York, NY 10003; (212) 529-9532.)

The Other Side of Faith
Seen from a first-person perspective, this film tells the true story of a remarkable Polish Catholic teenager who hid thirteen Jews in her attic. Filmed on location in Przemysl, Poland. (Available from Film and Video Foundation, 1800 K Street, Suite 1120, Washington, DC 20006; (202) 429-9320.)

Shoah
This film includes interviews with victims, perpetrators, and bystanders and takes viewers to camps, towns, and railways that were part of the Holocaust. (Available in most libraries and video stores.)

Weapons of the Spirit
This documentary tells the moving story of the French village of Le Chambon-sur-Lignon. The mostly Protestant townspeople there, under the leadership of Pastor André Trocmé, gave refuge to about 5,000 Jews during World War II. (Available from Zenger Video, 10200 Jefferson Boulevard, Room J, P. O. Box 802, Culver City, CA 90232; (800) 421-4246.)

Web Sites

Anti-Defamation League–Braun Holocaust Institute
http://www.adl.org/Braun/braun.htm

The Cybrary of the Holocaust
http://www.remember.org

Holocaust Education and Memorial Centre of Toronto
http://www.feduja.org

Museum of Tolerance
www.wiesenthal.com/mot/index.html

Simon Wiesenthal Center
http://www.wiesenthal.com/

United States Holocaust Memorial Museum
http://www.ushmm.org

Yad Vashem
http://www.yad-vashem.org.il

Index

About the Author

Esther Kustanowitz is a freelance writer who lives in New York. She is indebted to and inspired by those who shared their stories with her, and she thanks them from the bottom of her heart.

About the Series Editor

Yaffa Eliach is Professor of History and Literature in the Department of Judaic Studies at Brooklyn College. She founded and directed the Center for Holocaust Studies (now part of the Museum of Jewish Heritage—A Living Memorial to the Holocaust) and created the Tower of Life exhibit at the U.S. Holocaust Memorial Museum. Professor Eliach's book *There Once Was a World: A Nine Hundred Year Chronicle of the Shtetl of Eishyshok* was a finalist for the 1998 National Book Award for Nonfiction. She is also the author of *Hasidic Tales of the Holocaust; We Were Children Just Like You;* and *The Liberators: Eyewitness Accounts of the Liberation of Concentration Camps.*